From Robe to Crown
A Look Inside God's Wardrobe

By
Russell Hedley

ACKNOWLEDGMENTS

Illustrations by Hugh Burgess

Cover art by Abigail Hedley

Tale of Contents

AUTHOR'S NOTE

I am a fan of computer games, particularly when they involve a character navigating a story-driven adventure. Like most people, when they get stuck, I turn to online guides and walkthroughs. The guides will tell you how to progress your character or avatar; what to do next and where to get the best gear and clothing. This book then is a guide to the Christian character; it tells you how to begin your quest through gaining the garment of salvation and what else you will need to obtain on the way to winning the prize of the crown of life.

I hope this book will be useful to both the curious and the informed, the novice and the expert. The expert reader will be familiar with many of the scriptures quoted on these pages, but I pray that you will on reaching the end have made worthwhile modifications and tweaks to your character which will stand you in good stead on the journey of life. The novice may not know where to start in studying the bible so here for you are many scriptures like treasure chests waiting to be found and opened.

THE GARMENT OF SALVATION

I will greatly rejoice in the Lord; my soul shall exult in my God, for he has clothed me with the garments of salvation

(Isaiah 61 v 10)

Starting the Christian life involves acquiring a new set of clothes. We cannot venture out into the world naked, nor will we get far wearing the old clothes of our unsaved nature. The first item of clothing which we must obtain is the garment of salvation. It is, if you like, the undergarment over which all the other layers of clothing fit.

Acquiring the garment of salvation is straightforward, it just involves a step of faith. It means throwing out our old wardrobe and asking God for a new one. The act of turning our back on the things we used to wear and the things we used to do in them is what is meant by repentance. I am speaking figuratively, and no one should literally throw out all their old clothes, but what I am talking about is a change of heart. We become convinced that God knows what is best for our lives and we ask Him to take over. In response to our turning to Him and asking in faith – believing in Him – He gives us the garment of salvation.

Now the garment of salvation might not look very much, and it will often be covered over by various robes and armour, but it cost a lot. We get it for free, but Jesus paid a high price for it. It is His love gift to us, and He gives it to us without our having done anything to deserve it.

For God so loved the world that he gave his only begotten Son, that whoever believes in him should not perish but have eternal life

(John 3 v 16)

We call the free, or the undeserved, gift of God: the grace of God. A gracious giver is one who is constantly kind and generous, but the bible is very careful to remind us not to take this grace lightly (in vain).

Working together with him, then, we appeal to you not to receive the grace of God in vain

(2 Corinthians 6 v 1)

The way we take God's gift seriously is firstly through worship – there is a garment of praise as we shall see – and secondly by pledging our obedience, which is to say we become a follower or disciple of Jesus.

At first sight obedience does not seem very inviting, but the door to obedience is unlocked by a key called love. The greatest command of all is to love God, and the second is to love others.

You shall love the Lord your God with all your heart and with all your soul and with all your mind. This is the great and first commandment.

And the second is like it: You shall love your neighbour as yourself. On these two commandments depend all the Law and Prophets.

(Matthew 22 v 37-40)

In obeying the command to love we show ourselves to be true disciples of Jesus.

A new commandment I give you, that you love one another: just as I have loved you, you also are to love one another. By this all people will know that you are my disciples, if you have love for one another.

(John 13 v 34-35)

Now love may be shown in acts of kindness; in giving others our time, money, and patience, but there is one love command which is sometimes the hardest of all. It is the act of forgiving.

Be kind to one another, tenderhearted, forgiving one another, as God in Christ forgave you.

(Ephesians 4 v 32)

4

We must obey the command to forgive because forgiveness is embroidered on the garment of salvation.

For if you forgive other people when they sin against you, your heavenly Father will also forgive you. But if you do not forgive others their sins, your Father will not forgive your sins.

(Matthew 6 v 14-15 NIV)

One other important step in becoming a disciple is baptism.

Go therefore and make disciples of all nations, baptising them in the name of the Father and of the Son, and of the Holy Spirit, teaching them to observe all I have commanded you

(Matthew 28 v 19-20)

Baptism is important because it is a public declaration and we are surrounded by the church, which is our new family. It symbolises a new birth and represents the change that God has made in our hearts.

It could be said of baptism that we lay aside our old clothes, representing our old life and we emerge washed. and transformed wearing the garment of salvation.

A Prayer of Salvation:

Dear Lord Jesus, Son of God, thank you for dying on a cross for my sins. Please forgive me. I ask you to take these clothes of my old life, and to wash and clothe me anew with your salvation.

THE MANTLE OF PRAISE

The Lord God's spirit is upon me...To comfort all who mourn, to provide for Zion's mourners, to give them a crown in place of ashes, oil of joy in place of mourning, a mantle of praise in place of discouragement.

(Isaiah 61: v1 then verse 3 CEB)

A mantle is like a shawl or a cloak. So, let us think of it as something we can throw over our shoulders at any time and in any situation.

The mantle of praise is obtained by declaring the wonders of God. We can do this by speaking out or singing or just in the quietness of our own hearts. It can be done whenever we feel like it, but especially when we do not feel like it, when our spirit is "faint" or "downcast". We can give God praise at home, in the car on the way to work, in school or in the office. We can be alone or with others.

A good place to start is the Psalms:

Make a joyful noise to the Lord, all the earth!

Serve the Lord with gladness! Come into his presence with singing!

Know that the Lord, he is God! It is he who has made us, and we are his; we are his people and the sheep of his pasture.

Enter his gates with thanksgiving, and his courts with praise! Give thanks to him; bless his name!

For the Lord is good; his steadfast love endures forever, and his faithfulness to all generations.

(Psalm 100)

Notice that through praise and worship we are serving the Lord. It is also the way by which we come into His presence. It is an expression of joy and trust in Him. In difficult circumstances it rescues us from despondency and lifts our spirits.

Praise opens doors both to the spiritual realm, and the natural world as Paul and Silas found out when thrown in prison:

About midnight Paul and Silas were praying and singing hymns to God, and the prisoners were listening to them, and suddenly there was a great earthquake, so that the foundations of the prison were shaken. And immediately all the doors were opened, and everyone's bonds were unfastened.

(Acts 16 v 25-26)

In the face of a difficult situation or struggle praise and worship should be the first thing we turn to. In the Old Testament the choir went in front of the army.

And when he [Jehoshaphat] had taken counsel with the people, he appointed those who were to sing to the Lord, and praise him in holy attire, as they went before the army, and say:
"Give thanks to the Lord, for his steadfast love endures forever."

(2 Chronicles 20 v 21)

It is all too easy to forget or neglect to praise the Lord. It is important therefore to cultivate an attitude of praise, such that it comes spontaneously and naturally as the air we breathe.

Singing and making melody to the Lord with your heart, giving thanks always for everything to God the Father in the name of our Lord Jesus Christ

(Ephesians 5 v 19-20)

It is this expression of gratitude, which is at the heart of true worship, and makes the mantle of praise an essential accompaniment to the garment of salvation.

THE ROBE OF RIGHTEOUSNESS

…He has covered me with the robe of righteousness

(Isaiah 61 v 10)

The robe of righteousness represents the taking away of our sins; it is a priestly garment

Behold, I have taken your iniquity away from you, and I will clothe you with pure vestments

(Zechariah 3 v 4)

Let your priests be clothed with righteousness, and let your saints shout for joy

(Psalm 132 v 9)

The robe of righteousness is obtained through faith.

And be found in him, not having a righteousness of my own that comes from the law, but that which comes through faith in Christ, the righteousness from God that depends on faith
(Philippians 3 v 9)

We receive the garment of salvation when we first believe and turn to Christ, but we must also seek a garment made from fine linen.

His bride [the church] has made herself ready; it was granted her to clothe herself with fine linen, bright and pure, for the fine linen is the righteous deeds of the saints

(Revelation 19 v 7-8)

Thus, we see that our righteousness through faith produces righteous acts. It is the good tree bringing forth good fruit.

Abide in me, and I in you. As the branch cannot bear fruit by itself, unless it abides in the vine, neither can you, unless you abide in me.

(John 15 v 4)

It is our ongoing quest to remain, or abide (live), in Him. It cannot be emphasised enough that we must make a commitment. This is also why baptism is so important as it is our act of commitment to Him, and it allows Him to commit to us in a binding relationship. To be committed fully to Him it is important therefore to understand what it is we believe and what we mean by *His* righteousness.

The essence of the gospel – *the good news* – is that on the cross God oversaw a transaction. The transaction was that He (Jesus, the Son of God), who knew no sin, became sin, and we, who are sinners, became without sin. Through the forgiveness of sins, we are changed from evil to good, from unrighteous to righteous. This was not our doing, but it was done by God when He offered the perfect sacrifice for sin. Through Jesus sin was *atoned* for, the price paid. When you pay a price for something that was lost, you get it back, that is you *redeem* it.

For he [God] made him who knew no sin to be sin for us, that we might become the righteousness of God in him.

(2 Corinthians 5 v 21

Who himself bore our sins in his own body on the tree, that we, having died to sins, might live to righteousness -by whose stripes [wounds] you were healed.

(1 Peter 2 v 24)

The belief we are adhering to is that Jesus is the one true Son of God and that He lived as a man without sin. Most important is that this becomes our *confession*, meaning this is what we declare to others.

If you confess with your mouth, the Lord Jesus, and believe in your heart that God raised him from the dead, you will be saved.

(Romans 10 v 9)

When we confess Jesus as Lord of our life, the bible says we are stepping into Him, and becoming like Him. We commit to follow his example and to do what he says.

But put on [clothe yourself with] the Lord Jesus Christ, and make no provision for the flesh, to fulfil its lusts

(Romans 13 v 14)

Because of the blood that Jesus shed on the cross he has won for us the right to stand before God, clothed in His righteousness and not our own.

In him we have redemption through his blood, the forgiveness of sins, according to the riches of his grace.

(Ephesians 1 v 7)

We are the redeemed, whom God has forgiven our sins. He has given us a new beginning and the right to wear a robe without blemish: the robe of righteousness.

THE FULL ARMOUR OF GOD

Therefore, take up the whole armour of God, that you may be able to withstand in the evil day, and having done all, to stand firm.

Stand therefore, having fastened on the belt of truth, and having put on the breastplate of righteousness, and as shoes for your feet, having put on the readiness given by the gospel of peace. In all circumstances take up the shield of faith with which you can extinguish all the flaming darts of the evil one; and take the helmet of salvation, and the sword of the Spirit, which is the word of God.

(Ephesians 6 v 13-17)

The purpose of the armour of God is to stand and resist the devil. When the Apostle Paul wrote this he may have been thinking of a similar verse in the Old Testament: speaking of God:

He put on righteousness as a breastplate, and a helmet of salvation on his head; he put on garments of vengeance for clothing and wrapped himself in zeal as a cloak.

(Isaiah 59 v 17)

There is one difference: only God can inflict vengeance. But we see that we share the breastplate of righteousness and the helmet of salvation. This is important because they are *His* righteousness and *His* salvation. It could be said that we are wearing His coat of arms and we are identifiable

19

as belonging to His army. He is the captain, and we are the foot soldiers.

To win we need to learn how to fight and to do that we need to understand the enemy's strategy.

Be sober minded; be watchful. Your adversary the devil prowls around like a roaring lion, seeking someone to devour.

(1 Peter 5 v 8)

Lions hunt by chasing a fleeing victim. Never turn your back on a lion! The devil's prey is the truth; he seeks to destroy it.

You are of your father the devil, and your will is to do your father's desires. He was a murderer from the beginning, and does not stand in the truth, because there is no truth in him. When he lies, he speaks out of his own character, for he is a liar and the father of lies.

(John 8 v 44)

To live the truth, we wrap it tightly around our waist where it holds all the other armour in place. In defending the truth, the breastplate of righteousness protects our heart and in speaking the truth, we wield the powerful weapon of the sword of the Spirit.

For the word of God is living and active, sharper than any two-edged sword, piercing to the division of soul and spirit, of joints and of marrow, and discerning the thoughts and intentions of the heart.

(Hebrews 4 v 12)

Satan is also described as "the accuser of the brethren" (Revelation 12 v 7-12). We see an example of this in the Old Testament in the life of Joshua, the high priest.

Then he showed me Joshua the high priest standing before the angel of the Lord, and Satan standing at his right hand to accuse him.

(Zechariah 3 v 1)

Satan brings accusations, slander, and fault-finding; these are his "flaming darts". His purpose is to bring guilt and condemnation. Whereas the Holy Spirit may convict us of sin, we know God is faithful to forgive us (this is the truth), but when the devil brings condemnation (this is the lie) it leads to hopelessness and despair. If we are not careful – *be watchful!* – the accusations result in an attack on our mind, and we doubt our salvation. The helmet of salvation protects and guards us from doubting thoughts

If we read on in Zechariah, we see the Lord's response to the devil's accusations against Joshua.

And the Lord said to Satan, "The Lord rebuke you, O Satan! The Lord who has chosen Jerusalem rebuke you! Is not this [man] a brand snatched from the fire?" Now Joshua was standing before the angel clothed with filthy garments. And the angel said to those who were standing before him, "Remove the filthy garments from him." And to him he said, "Behold, I have taken your iniquity away from you, and I will clothe you with pure vestments.

(Zechariah 3 v 2-4)

The devil would have us keep our filthy clothes, whereas the truth is that our sins are forgiven, and God gives us pure, white robes to wear.

Then one of the elders addressed me, saying, "Who are these, clothed in white robes, and from where have they come?" I said to him, "Sir, you know." And he said to me, "These are the ones coming out of the great tribulation. They have washed their robes and made them white in the blood of the Lamb.

(Revelation 7 v 13-14)

Our footwear is for crushing Satan under our feet.

For your obedience is known to all, so that I rejoice over you, but I want you to be wise as to what is good and innocent as to what is evil. The God of peace will soon crush Satan under your feet.

(Romans 16 v 19-20)

The gospel of peace is the truth of our reconciliation with God. In becoming children of God, we become brothers and sisters in God's family. It is this unity that the devil seeks to undermine by bringing argument and division. We see this in the preceding verses in Romans chapter 16.

I appeal to you, brothers, to watch out for those who cause divisions and create obstacles, contrary to the doctrine that you have been taught; avoid them. For such persons do not serve our Lord Christ, but their own appetites, and by smooth talk and flattery they deceive the hearts of the naive.

(Romans 16 v 17-18)

The soldier will not stand for long if his feet are on slippery ground. He needs to be prepared (ready) and alert to things which seek to cause offense and argument. If we are not careful and fully committed to the gospel of peace we fall into the devil's trap.

The gospel of peace is the secure footing on which the armour of God stands

And the peace of God, which surpasses all understanding will guard your hearts and your minds in Christ Jesus.

(Philippians 4 v 7)

THE GARB OF HUMILITY

Clothe yourselves, all of you, with humility toward one another, for
'God opposes the proud but gives grace to the humble'

(1 Peter 5 v 5)

This is the very garment worn by Jesus Himself

[Jesus] emptied himself, by taking the form of a servant, being born in the likeness of men. And being found in human form, he humbled himself by becoming obedient to the point of death on a cross.

(Philippians 2 v 7-8)

The garment of humility is woven from service and seamed with obedience. Jesus taught his disciples this when he washed their feet:

He laid aside his outer garments, and taking a towel, tied it around his waist

(John 13 v 4)

When he had washed their feet and put on his outer garments and resumed his place, he said to them, "Do you understand what I have done to you? You call me Teacher and Lord, and you are right, for so I am. If I then, your Lord and Teacher, have washed your feet, you also ought to wash one another's feet. For I have given you an example, that you also should do just as I have done to you"

(John 13 v 12-15)

Jesus set an example and gave a command: *wash one another's feet*. There cannot be a humbler garment than a towel but with it we provide a great service to one another and show ourselves to be true disciples of Jesus. Although the full armour of God may be glorious and powerful it does not lend itself easily to the washing of feet and when wearing it, we must not lose sight of the humble servant we are meant to be. This is the danger of pride, and it is pride that Jesus was warning his disciples to be on guard against.

We wash one another's feet by loving them, by putting them before ourselves and through many acts of kindness. In this way we serve the Lord.

Then the King will say to those on his right, 'Come, you who are blessed by my Father, inherit the kingdom prepared for you from the foundation of the world. For I was hungry and you gave me food; I was thirsty and you gave me drink; I was a stranger and you welcomed me, I was naked and you clothed me, I was sick and you visited me, I was in prison and you came to Me.' Then the righteous will answer him, saying, 'Lord when did we see you hungry and feed you, or thirsty and give you drink? And when did we see you a stranger and welcome you, or naked and clothe you?' And the King will answer them, 'Truly, I say to you, as you did it to one of the least of these my brothers, you did it to me'"

(Matthew 25 v 34-40)

Humility guides us to serve the least, and love to find the lost; but pride blinds us to the needs of both.

THE CROWN OF LIFE

Be faithful unto death, and I will give you the crown of life.

(Revelation 2 v 10)

Blessed is the man who remains steadfast under trial, for when he has stood the test he will receive the crown of life, which God has promised to those who love him.

(James 1 v 12)

To be steadfast means to hold steady, remain faithful, stay on course. The way to do this is to not lose sight of the ultimate prize, which is eternal life that God promises to those who love him.

The Lord is not slow to fulfil his promise as some count slowness, but is patient toward you, not wishing that any should perish, but that all should reach repentance.

(2 Peter 3 v 9)

A crown symbolizes glory and honour. A *crowning glory* is an ultimate achievement. The apostle Paul likened life to running a race.

Therefore, since we are surrounded by so great a cloud of witnesses, let us also lay aside every weight, and sin which clings so closely, and let us run with endurance the race that is set before us, looking to Jesus, the founder and perfector of our faith, who for the joy set before him endured the cross, despising the shame and is seated at the right hand of the throne of God.

(Hebrews 12 v 1-2)

We see a picture of heaven cheering us on – the *cloud of witnesses* – with Jesus as our coach and role-model; waiting for us to cross the line, seated at the *right hand of the throne of God.*

I have fought the good fight, I have finished the race, I have kept the faith. Henceforth, there is laid up for me the crown of righteousness, which the Lord, the righteous Judge, will give me on that day, and not only to me but also to all who have loved his appearing.

(2 Timothy 4 v 7-8)

Although Jesus suffered, he looked forward with joy to the glory that would be given to those who trust Him.

*In bringing many sons and daughters to glory, it was fitting that God,
for whom and through whom everything exists should make the
pioneer of their salvation perfect through what he suffered*

(Hebrews 2 v 10 NIV)

In our quest for the crown of life therefore, we are called to
be like Jesus in our resolve and determination and to
eagerly anticipate God's reward.

*He will render each one according to his works: to those who by
patience in well-doing seek for glory and honour and immortality, he
will give eternal life; but for those who are self-seeking and do not obey
the truth, but obey unrighteousness, there will be wrath and fury.*

(Romans 2 v 6-8)

Patience is the ability to wait; to continue doing something
despite difficulties, or to suffer without complaining or
becoming annoyed. We will need this if we are to obtain
the crown of life because the world is full of challenges.

*I have said these things to you, that in me you may have peace. In the
world you will have tribulation. But take heart; I have overcome the
world.*

(John 16 v 33)

*In this you rejoice, though now for a little while, if necessary, you have
been grieved by various trials, so that the tested genuineness of your*

faith — more precious than gold that perishes though it is tested by fire — may be found to result in praise and glory and honour at the revelation of Jesus Christ.

(1 Peter 1v 6-7)

Our endurance and faith are in hope of the revealing (appearing) of Jesus Christ in His authority and glory. This hope is not wishful thinking — it is a fervent expectation, an eager anticipation that one day we will behold the glory of God and live with Him forever. Our destiny is eternity.

Through him we have also obtained access by faith into this grace in which we stand, and we rejoice in hope of the glory of God. Not only that, but we rejoice in our sufferings, knowing that suffering produces endurance, and endurance produces character, and character produces hope, and hope does not put us to shame, because God's love has been poured into our hearts through the Holy Spirit who has been given us.

(Romans 5 v 2-5)

God has not left us without a Helper in our quest for the crown of life. He has given us the gift of the Holy Spirit.

But the Helper, the Holy Spirit, whom the Father will send in my name, he will teach you all things and bring to your remembrance all that I have said to you.

(John 14 v 26)

He has also given us His Word, which we must not neglect to study.

All Scripture is breathed out by God and profitable for teaching, for reproof, for correction, and for training in righteousness.

(2 Timothy 3 v16)

I have given them your word, and the world has hated them because they are not of the world. I do not ask that you take them out of the world, but that you keep them from the evil one.

(John 17 v 14-15)

As we have seen the evil one is Satan, the accuser, and it is him we must overcome. There are two things which enable us to overcome: the blood of Jesus and our testimony.

And they have conquered him by the blood of the lamb and by the word of their testimony, for they loved not their lives even unto death

(Revelation 12 v 11)

The Blood of the Lamb is our sanctification. In the Old Testament the priests would sprinkle the blood of sacrificed animals on the altar to make it holy. To be holy (sanctified) means set apart; separated for God's use. We have been made holy by the blood of Jesus, and it is this about which we testify. When a person testifies, they are acting as a witness – they are giving evidence. To do this we need but answer one simple question.

He said to them, "But who do you say that I am?"

(Matthew 16 v 15)

As with Peter we reply:

"You are the Christ, the Son of the living God"

(Matthew 16 v 16)

FINAL WORD

The bible is full of encouragement. I hope that if you have been blessed by this book you will pass it on to somebody else.

However, if you are feeling that your armour is a little tarnished; that the helmet of salvation is rather skewed on your head, or that the mantle of praise has fallen off your shoulders, I have a final word: God is in the restoration business. If you let Him, He will have that shield of faith polished up and the robe of righteousness whiter than white. You see He loves you. You just have to trust Him because He is able to do more than we can think or imagine. Take hold of this word and believe that He *is able* and when you stand before Him it will be with great joy.

Now to him who is able to keep you from stumbling and to present you blameless before the presence of his glory with great joy, to the only God, our Saviour, through Jesus Christ our Lord, be glory, majesty, dominion, and authority, before all time and now and forever.

Amen

(Jude 1 v 24-25)

Printed in Great Britain
by Amazon

80401469R00031